Tales of Old

Other counties in this series include:

Tales of Old Cheshire

Carole Sexton

With illustrations by Don Osmond

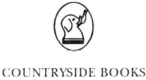

COUNTRYSIDE BOOKS
NEWBURY, BERKSHIRE

First published 1995
© Carole Sexton 1995
Reprinted 2001
This new edition 2011

COUNTRYSIDE BOOKS
3 Catherine Road
Newbury, Berkshire

To view our complete range of books,
please visit us at
www.countrysidebooks.co.uk

ISBN 978 1 84674 246 0

To my parents,
Mary and John Sexton

Cover designed by Peter Davies, Nautilus Design
Produced through MRM Associates Ltd., Reading
Printed by Information Press, Oxford

Contents

CONTENTS

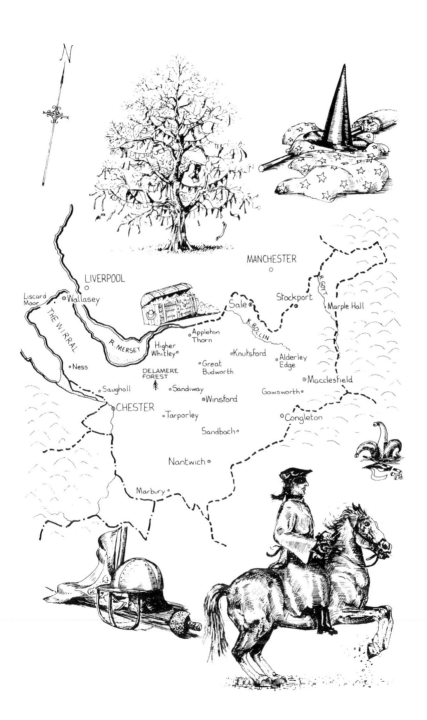

N

MANCHESTER

LIVERPOOL

Liscard
Moor
Wallasey

THE WIRRAL

R. MERSEY

Ness

DELAMERE
FOREST

Saughall

CHESTER

Tarporley

Nantwich

Marbury

Sale

Stockport

Marple Hall

R. GOYT

R. BOLLIN

Appleton
Thorn

Higher
Whitley

Knutsford

Alderley
Edge

Great
Budworth

Macclesfield

Sandiway

Winsford

Gawsworth

Congleton

Sandbach

'Gentleman Higgins'

Knutsford can be justly proud of its famous literary daughter Mrs Elizabeth Gaskell who, although born in London, grew up in the Cheshire town which is the setting for her famous novel *Cranford*.

However, not all residents are remembered as favourably as the popular Victorian novelist. Take for instance a certain Edward Higgins, gentleman of Knutsford by day, notorious highwayman and burglar after dark.

'Gentleman Higgins' as he was known, led a colourful life before arriving in Cheshire. He narrowly escaped hanging for sheep-stealing at Worcester in 1752, only to be later sentenced to transportation after being found guilty of housebreaking. Once in America he was soon up to his old tricks, and after breaking into a house in Boston he used the proceeds of the raid to pay for a passage back to England, long before his seven year exile was up.

After a short spell living in Manchester Higgins settled in Knutsford, marrying a respectable young lady called Katherine Birtles on 21st April 1757. The union produced five children, and the former rogue seemed to have settled down to the life of an exemplary country gentleman. Higgins and his wife were soon on excellent terms with the local gentry, finding themselves welcomed in all the best homes in the district.

Even when an expensive snuff-box disappeared while Edward was paying a call at Oulton Park, the home of Mr Egerton, no one suspected the handsome, charming Mr Higgins – why should they? However, as a local writer Henry Green later declared, at this time our hero was not limiting himself to petty theft. While hunting with the aristocracy in the morning, dining with them in the afternoon he was also making himself 'familiar with their plate chests by night'.

As well as house-breaking, Edward was abroad at night, masked and armed with a pistol, holding up the coaches of his friends. One evening he left a ball early intending to relieve Lady Warburton of her jewels. The highwayman followed his would-be victim along the road to Arley; however his plan had to be abandoned when the lady leaned out of her coach window and recognising him, for he was as yet unmasked, called out 'Good evening, Mr Higgins'.

To all he seemed a genial, popular, county squire. Not even his wife and children suspected he was leading a double life. Edward Higgins actually muffled his horse's hooves with woollen socks so as not to wake his family and alert them to his nocturnal activities. Katherine believed their income derived from property, as her husband disappeared for a month or so each year, supposedly to collect rents. In fact he travelled as far afield as Bristol, Gloucester and South Wales on house-breaking sorties.

Higgins' crimes gradually became more audacious and ruthless. One day when he was raiding a house in Stanley Street, Chester, he found himself in the bedroom of a young lady who suddenly awoke. Seeing a shadowy figure at her dressing-table she mistook the intruder for a maid putting away her jewellery. 'Leave that until morning, Mary', she called before turning over and going back to sleep. This was fortunate indeed, because Higgins later admitted he would not have hesitated to kill the girl if she had seen his face. Later he was to confess to having committed several murders.

As he had escaped detection for so long, Higgins must have felt he was untouchable. It was this belief, coupled with a curious desire for recognition that led to his downfall. While with his Knutsford friends he began discussing in detail crimes he himself had committed. His considerable knowledge of events that had taken place many miles away began to arouse suspicion amongst some of his listeners, and when he showed first-hand intelligence about the murder of a wealthy widow and her maid during a robbery in Bristol, events came to a head. News of this outrage had yet to reach Knutsford and local people were puzzled by Higgins' prior knowledge of the dreadful crimes.

The local constable was alerted, but Edward Higgins must have realised he had betrayed himself and fled before he could be arrested.

Ever resourceful, he remained free for another year or so, once again living the life of a gentleman – although without his family – near Bristol. But time was running out and when Higgins crossed into South Wales he was finally caught red-handed in the act of breaking into a house in Carmarthen.

After a trial at which he protested his innocence throughout, Gentleman Higgins was sentenced to death for his many crimes. This audacious felon was not beaten yet however, and when a reprieve arrived addressed to the Sheriff of Carmarthen it seemed he had cheated justice once again. His daring ruse might have worked, but a sharp-eyed official noticed the document had a local postmark, rather than the correct London cancel. Higgins had paid a friend to send the bogus missive.

Higgins is said to have received the news from the Sheriff of the failure of his ruse and consequently his impending execution with 'inconceivable insolence', and to have subjected the sheriff to the most abusive language. Despite screamed threats that he would fight to the death rather than be brought to the gallows, on 7th November 1767, Edward Higgins went quietly enough. It was reported he died in a 'sullen manner', his long career of crime over at last.

As Higgins once occupied the house next door to Elizabeth Gaskell's aunts, she must have heard tales of this notorious former tenant as she grew up. She was influenced enough to write about him in her *Squires Tale*, and the memory of the 'gentleman' lives on as a character in the Knutsford Royal May procession.

'Cheshire's Own Prophet'

The ability to foretell the future is a gift possessed by very few people. Among these, surely one of the strangest was 'Cheshire's Own Prophet', Robert Nixon.

Born the son of a tenant farmer during the final decade of the 16th century in the parish of Over, near Winsford, he began his working life as a farm labourer for the Cholmondeley family. According to contemporary descriptions it appears that Robert Nixon was little short of an idiot. He is said to have been a 'short squat fellow' with 'a great head and goggle eyes', and he dribbled on the rare occasions that he spoke adding to the impression of his imbecility.

Apart from his appearance Nixon was unpopular amongst his fellows both for his surly manner and extreme greed. Given the opportunity he would eat a whole shoulder of mutton at one sitting, and then finish off the meal with bread and cheese.

This behaviour paled into insignificance in comparison to what occurred while he was employed as a ploughman. Nixon developed the rather alarming tendency to stop in the middle of a field in a trance-like state and make pronouncements in a voice most unlike his own. These meant little at the time, but apparently they prophesied great events that would take place long after Nixon's death.

One day Robert ceased work and announced:

> 'If the favourite of a king shall be slain,
> The master's head shall be cleft in twain.'

Although mystifying at the time this was obviously a reference to the assassination of the 1st Duke of Buckingham in 1628 and the execution of Charles I in 1649.

The English Civil War was forecast in the following terms:

'Great wars and a pressing of soldiers
But at last clubs and clouted shoes shall carry the day.'

Some other events he foresaw included the Restoration of Charles II, the Great Fire of London and the Plague, and also the French Revolution. A prediction nearer to home was that the wall of Vale Royal Abbey would collapse, which it did in 1688. Nixon also foretold that his own death would be due to starvation. This must have seemed most unlikely to those who knew of his voracious appetite.

Despite the cryptic nature of his sayings, they were recognised as being of importance and by his early twenties the prophet's fame had spread as far as London. King James I, a superstitious man with a considerable interest in the supernatural, sent for Robert. The king must have been surprised when he saw this odd-looking youth from the depths of the Cheshire countryside, and probably for this reason alone he decided to test him. The monarch hid a valuable diamond ring, claiming to have recently lost it, and requested Robert to find it. Nixon immediately replied 'He who hideth can find'.

The king was suitably impressed and gave Nixon the freedom of his palaces, also ordering that his utterances be recorded for posterity. The hospitality was liberally enjoyed by Robert who had not lost his love of fine food and drink. He now spent most of his free time alternating between the royal wine cellars and the kitchens where he sampled the dishes being prepared, often passing critical remarks as to their quality. As can be imagined this did not endear him to the king's servants.

One day when the king was preparing to go on a hunting trip, intending to be away several days, Nixon ran to him begging not to be left behind with the servants who so disliked him. James laughed, telling him not to worry and that he would soon return. However, so insistent was Robert that his royal master relented and appointed an official to care for him.

Shortly afterwards James must have forgotten his promise for he summoned the steward to attend him on other duties at Hampton Court. The steward was now faced with a dilemma – he could not question the royal command but the prophet's unpopularity was such that he feared for Nixon's safety if he was left to the mercy of the royal household's staff. It was for this reason he took the unusual decision to lock the prophet in a spacious cupboard during his enforced absence. Not expecting to be away for more than a day or so the steward felt it unnecessary to leave the grossly overweight Nixon any food.

When he returned after a delay of several days, the steward hurried to release his captive, expecting to find an irate and presumably hungry prophet. He must have had a nasty shock when he opened the door and the body of Robert Nixon slumped out on to the floor.

The doctors declared the cause of death to be starvation (and, presumably, dehydration), although by rights a young man of his generous proportions should have been able to survive for the relatively short period that he was denied food and water.

Robert Nixon's bizarre death remains as much a mystery as his strange life. How was this simple, illiterate countryman able to utter such articulate and seemingly prophetic statements? These prophecies, although somewhat vague, bear sufficient similarity to subsequent events to identify them with great occurrences. Why such a man as Nixon should have become a vehicle for prophecy remains an enigma.

The Wizard of Alderley Edge

L ooking at the great 600 ft high brooding mound that is Alderley Edge, it's hardly surprising that as well as giving the nearby town its name, the hill has also gained a reputation as the most magical and mysterious area of Cheshire.

Here you feel that perhaps the thin veil separating past and present could easily be lifted, revealing the ancient men who mined copper on its slopes and lit pagan bonfires on the summit. Certainly the farmer from Mobberley who set off to Macclesfield market one day in the year 1695 would have known of the local legends that the Edge was a haunt of witches and the scene of supernatural happenings. However, nothing could have prepared him for the wonders he was about to experience.

In the light of early morning the man passed by the lower wooded slopes of the hill leading the fine white horse that he intended to sell that day. He saw no reason to be alarmed when he was approached by a very old man leaning heavily on a staff. But he was astonished when after wishing him good day, this shabbily dressed ancient offered to buy the animal.

The appearance of the man suggested he would not be able to offer a very good price, and as the farmer believed that a better deal could be negotiated in town, he refused. The old man then predicted that he would not succeed in selling the horse at market, and told him they would meet again that evening. The farmer laughed and went on his way, dismissing the old chap as an eccentric. After all, why would he want such a horse?

Much to the seller's surprise, and despite several promising enquiries he did not manage to clinch a sale, and he was forced to set off for home disappointed. As he returned, following the same route, the old man reappeared as promised, and without speaking a word motioned the farmer to follow him.

Leading his animal the farmer accompanied this strange figure almost against his will. It was as though some unseen force was propelling him forward.

Together they passed a rock called Stormy Point and finally stopped before the blank face of Castle Rock, a sandstone cliff forming the eastern side of the Edge. The farmer must have known something momentous was about to happen when a door suddenly appeared in what a few seconds before had been solid rock. The old man struck the entrance with his staff, and it swung open to reveal a deep cave.

When his eyes had grown accustomed to the dark, the visitor was amazed to see a vast number of apparently sleeping men in full armour, complete with swords and shields. They lay on slabs of stone and by their sides, also in the same state of suspended animation, were mighty horses of war. As if this was not enough, how the farmer must have marvelled at the sight of numerous piles of large gold coins scattered around the floor.

The ancient one now explained that these sleeping warriors were none other than King Arthur and the men of Camelot who waited in their secret chamber until such time as their country had need of them. Then they would rise up as the Nation's saviours, defeating her enemies in one last great conflict. The narrator indicated a knight resplendent in gold armour, this he said was Arthur himself, and he had need of a suitable mount on which to lead his men.

Now, belatedly, it dawned on the open-mouthed farmer that his guide on this journey and the teller of this fantastic tale, was none other than Arthur's venerable mentor, the magician Merlin. This immortal figure now instructed him to

17

take what payment he required from the heaps of gold. Hardly taking his eyes off the slumbering knights, he did what he was told and scooped up in his hat as much gold as he could carry away with him, and withdrew hastily from the wizard's lair. Now much richer than after a thousand visits to Macclesfield market, the farmer made his way back down the mountain trail and back to his farm.

Some of the farmer's neighbours were sceptical when he related his experiences but they could not deny his sudden wealth and complete change of circumstances.

Today Alderley Edge is a popular spot with visitors who can enjoy a drink at the Wizard Inn while admiring fine views of the Cheshire plain and distant Pennines. However, search as they might, no one has ever succeeded in finding Arthur's cave or discovering his treasure. Merlin himself still keeps the secret.

The Wise Woman
of Delamere Forest

Delamere forest is a place of great natural beauty
extremely popular with people seeking a pleasant and
peaceful day of leisure. Of the numerous visitors who enjoy
what the forest has to offer very few would choose to set up
home in this remote rural spot. However, in 1815, this is
exactly what Maria Ann Hollingsworth did.

The daughter of a Lutheran clergyman Maria was an
educated woman of some refinement who, despite suffering
great poverty still showed traces of having been a great
beauty. Born in Leuwarden, West Friesland in 1765, as a
young woman she had married a British soldier, a member of
an expeditionary force sent to Germany to assist in fighting
the French. Maria and their two children, a son and
daughter, followed the army until her husband fell at the
battle of Bergen-Op-Zoom in 1814.

Disowned by her strict family and alone in the world Maria
apprenticed her young son to a carpenter in Hanover,
believing this to be the best course to secure him a future.
Then mother and daughter travelled to England after Maria
was awarded a small pension and the protection of Queen
Charlotte, wife of George III. The queen would have sym-
pathised with this woman whose husband had been killed
fighting for his country, and though there is no evidence that
they had ever met, Maria wrote to many influential people,
and it is possible that Charlotte awarded the pension in
response to such a letter.

Overland they made the journey in a covered donkey cart

which offered them shelter at night. The two goats that accompanied them provided milk for their sustenance during the long journey.

Life was hard for the pair as they were constantly moved on by parish officials who did not want an added financial burden. The Poor Law Act of Settlement (1622) permitted overseers to compel vagrants not born in that parish to return to their native parish, and no one was prepared to accept a foreign-born couple. They need not have worried, Maria herself did not wish to be a liability, for as she states in a letter to Lady Thumley, a prominent local landowner: 'I never intend to submyt to Parish keeping'.

As they could not find unenclosed land on which to settle the travellers decided to seek a passage to America. It was while they were passing through Delamere on their way to Liverpool that Maria had a change of heart. The solitude offered by the area so appealed to both mother and daughter that Maria addressed a humble plea for permission to settle, outlined in a letter to Lady Thumley dated 17th July 1815. 'I am at present at your property, namely Oakmere', and after describing her situation, Maria asked for 'some waste ground for then I can live and provide for myself'.

Maria appealed to Lady Thumley presumably because she felt another woman would sympathise with her plight. However, after Lady Thumley had shown him the letter it was Thomas Cholmondeley who eventually agreed that Maria and her daughter might live on his land, even though their choice of dwelling probably surprised him. Maria took advantage of two whale ribs erected on a bank near Oakmere by Philip Egerton of Oulton as a souvenir of his travels. She set about turning these into a 'novel habitacion' some eight ft by ten ft in width and five ft high, with walls constructed of sods of earth and a roof of tree branches. An enclosed area surrounding their home of one and a half acres served them to grow produce and keep chickens.

As word got around of the new residents and their strange cottage, visitors began to arrive. These callers found Maria –

or Mary Ann as she became known – a charming and intelligent woman who despite her love of solitude also enjoyed the occasional company. One of the reasons folk from near and far frequented Maria's home was her growing reputation as a wise woman. They came to seek her advice as well as to listen to her tales of far away lands.

There were some less enlightened people who suspected that her knowledge and wisdom coupled with an unusual life-style indicated witchcraft, and wild stories did circulate about her. But the majority of her callers were friendly and many contributed small amounts of money to assist the family budget. Maria also earned a little by teaching some of the local children – along with her daughter – to read and write in English, French and German. In time she was able to make improvements to their house, adding turf walls, a door and casement windows. When their donkey died this faithful old servant continued to be useful, as its hide was stretched over the roof to keep out the rain.

In 1820 Maria was excited to receive a letter from her son to say he soon intended to visit them. He was to sail from Hamburg to Liverpool, and each day mother and daughter would take turns to watch the road by which he would arrive.

One day Maria saw a man approaching who from the distance she thought might be her son. She was not sure, as it had been six years since they parted, and then he had been only a boy. To her surprise the man stopped at a roadside cottage, possibly to ask the way. Maria was concerned at this because the man who lived there had rather a bad reputation. After a vigil of several hours there was still no sign of the traveller, and Maria became more and more worried. As night fell she crept to the cottage to investigate and was horrified to see the owner and his son leave, carrying a large sack. She followed, and witnessed them throw their burden into the mere. The sack would not sink and, cursing foully, the two men removed it and conveyed the obviously heavy object back to their cottage. They disappeared inside and after returning with spades they went to the rear of the house.

The distraught mother hurried to Mr Wilbraham, the local magistrate, who promised to investigate immediately, but no body was ever found, and the men would give no explanation for what Maria believed she had witnessed. Some weeks later Wilbraham told her that he had traced her son and that in fact he had never left Hanover.

Shortly afterwards a young man did arrive at Maria's cottage, and although mother and daughter accepted him, it was without enthusiasm. Maria still could not rid herself of the belief that the mysterious stranger – who may or may not have met an untimely end – was truly her son, and that there had been some form of official cover-up.

The charms of Delamere had now faded for the pair, and when her daughter married Maria accepted a place in the Dutch Almhouses in London where she peacefully ended her days.

The Last Jester

The sleepy Cheshire village of Gawsworth might not seem the most likely place to have produced the country's last professional jester. But it was indeed here that the holder of that title, Samuel 'Maggotty' Johnson, was born in 1691.

Brought up in the shadow of the lovely Tudor manor house, Gawsworth Hall, the birthplace of Mary Fitton – reputedly the dark lady of Shakespeare's later sonnets – when he was past boyhood Samuel set off to make his fortune in London.

He already had a rudimental knowledge of music and during the latter years of Queen Anne's reign he continued the study of his chosen craft in numerous London playhouses. So adept did he become that Samuel impressed members of noble families who invited him to perform at their homes. This led to his introduction to the royal court, where he entertained the most exalted in the land. Under his professional name 'Lord Flame', Samuel told witty stories and performed acrobatic tricks, he was particularly adept at stilt-walking. His talents did not end there, an accomplished musician, he also taught dancing to the children of the nobility at the courts of Anne and her successor German George I. Unfortunately the Hanoverian monarch spoke no English, so unable fully to appreciate Samuel's humour, and possibly that is why Mr Johnson turned his talents to play-writing.

Though 'Maggotty' did not achieve the renown of his namesake Dr Samuel Johnson, he was an actor and poet of considerable ability. He wrote and performed in *Hurlothrumbo* (1729), a tale of the supernatural which ran for 30 successive nights at the Haymarket Theatre, London. The play was described by his contemporary John Byrom (who wrote the epilogue) as being full of 'oddities, out-of-the-waynesses, flights, madness, comicalities etc'.

Despite this triumph on the London stage, Gawsworth was always close to Samuel's heart. On one occasion he returned for a visit bringing with him a group of his actor friends. The rural peace must have been rudely shattered by the carousing thespians who got drunk whenever the opportunity arose. One evening Samuel himself became so incapable that his friends put him in the stocks and left him there overnight. Their victim did not appreciate the joke. So strongly did Samuel feel that his reputation was damaged that he declared to a friend 'I will have to make a retreat from beloved Gawsworth and leave no trace behind.' This must have been said at the height of his embarrassment, as return he did.

Despite further attempts at writing for the stage, he never repeated his earlier success. Eventually Samuel Johnson retired to Gawsworth, where the Earl of Harrington presented him with a small house. Here he lived comfortably, receiving pensions from several wealthy patrons who probably remembered their old dancing master with affection.

It seems that by now Samuel had become rather eccentric, for when the Earl's steward brought his allowances, he would have to present them formally with the words 'My Lord, I have brought you your rents.' Apparently by now the former jester really believed he was 'Lord Flame', a nobleman accepting his just levies.

It was this eccentricity that led to the locals nicknaming their illustrious neighbour 'Maggotty', meaning in Cheshire dialect not quite right in the head. To his face, however, they doffed their caps respectfully to 'his Lordship'.

'Maggotty' appeared to confirm the villagers' opinion of him when on his death-bed he demanded burial, not in the churchyard, but in a local copse. This wish was granted, and his grave can still be visited in a spinney that bears the name

'Maggotty's Wood', just off the main Macclesfield to Congleton road.

Samuel Johnson composed his own rather strange epitaph, which might explain his desire for a secluded burial place, or was he perhaps playing the jester to the end?

'That when he rose again, laid here above,
No friend and he should quarrel for a bone,
Thinking that where some old lame gossip nigh,
She possibly might take his leg or thigh.'

Whatever his fears were, he rests undisturbed, but his presence is still to be felt in the district. At Gawsworth Hall his fiddle hangs on display, and his ghost is said to caper along the lanes on warm summer evenings.

King Charles's Tower

Unlike Cromwellian Nantwich, Chester remained staunchly loyal to the Crown during England's Civil War. In recognition of their allegiance Charles I visited the city in 1642, immediately after raising his standard at Nottingham, and was met with a rousingly enthusiastic welcome from the townspeople.

Following the decisive defeat at Naseby in June 1645 the war was progressing badly for the Royalist cause, and by the autumn of that year Chester itself was besieged and threatened from all sides. On receiving the news the king, who had been lodging at Chirk Castle in North Wales on his way to Scotland, decided to break his journey in order to offer much needed military assistance and to strengthen the citizens' resolve.

When it became known Charles was to come to Chester's aid, Sir Francis Gamul, a former mayor and member of an illustrious local family, put his Lower Bridge Street home at the king's disposal. Charles duly arrived on 24th September with half his army, and gained entry into the city.

The remainder of the troops, under Sir Marmaduke Langdale, travelled via Holt with the intention of approaching Chester from the rear. The plan was that Langdale – nicknamed the 'Ghost' because of his extremely slim build – should attack from the rear, while Charles and his men launched a frontal assault from the city.

At first the plan seemed to be working; Langdale engaged the Parliamentarian forces under General Poyntz at Rowton Moor some two miles outside the town. The Cavaliers fought well, holding their own, but the commander became increasingly concerned when there was no sign of Charles' expected force.

Sir Marmaduke realised he needed to send an urgent message to his king, but how to do so proved a problem as the suburbs were full of enemy soldiers. In the hope that his expert knowledge of the area would prove useful, Langdale then approached Sir Geoffrey Shakerley, a local man from Lower Peover who was a colonel attached to Prince Rupert's cavalry.

This courageous gentleman volunteered to act as messenger. From Handbridge he surveyed the banks of the River Dee seeking a way to safely reach Charles. Then, spotting a tub normally used in the slaughter of pigs, an idea occurred to him. Acquiring a 'batting staff', a wooden pole used in the manufacture of coarse linen, Shakerley pushed the tub into the river. With his servant beside him and his horse swimming alongside, this enterprising soldier rowed the makeshift vessel to the opposite shore. On reaching the Chester side, Sir Geoffrey disclosed his identity to the guards at the Bridge Gate, and he was brought into the king's presence within 15 minutes of leaving Handbridge.

Unfortunately this valiant action was in vain. Always an indecisive man, for some inexplicable reason Charles delayed sending the urgently needed help. The troops from Chester were not dispatched until six hours after the battle was lost.

Sporadic skirmishes continued for many hours, then on 27th September, from the Phoenix Tower situated on the city walls, Charles witnessed the stragglers from Langdale's army desperately fleeing to safety. To commemorate this event the building was renamed King Charles' Tower, the title it still bears today.

Charles later moved to the roof of the cathedral for a better view, and while he stood there a musket shot fired from St John the Baptist's church struck and killed a captain standing next to him. The king was advised by an anxious Sir Francis to retire to Gamul House for his own well being.

After instructing the civic leaders to surrender a few days after he had gone the following day Charles left the city to its fate, galloping with his remaining men over the Old Dee Bridge. The Cestrains were made of sterner stuff than their king, and held out until 3rd February of the following year, only giving up when at the point of starvation.

Their struggle had been in vain; the following year Charles was handed over to Parliament by the Scots, and the first phase of the Civil War was over.

The Peppergate
Elopement

Just as today, medieval Chester was surrounded by protective walls. Each day hundreds of visitors and Cestrians alike have used its various gateways, entrances like the small ancient opening beside the modern Newgate built in 1938. But this entrance, the Peppergate, differs from its fellows for it has the distinction of bearing silent witness to Chester's most famous elopement.

During the reign of Elizabeth I a mayor of Chester, one Alderman Ralph Aldersey, had a beautiful daughter called Ellen. It is not surprising that such a leading citizen should want an excellent marriage for his only child, and to this end he bethrothed her to a wealthy suitor some years her senior. Though her father's choice for her, Ellen wanted nothing to do with him, for she was in love with a penniless young Welsh armourer called Luke.

When Alderman Aldersey found out about the association he determined that the couple should not be allowed to meet. To ensure no assignations took place he kept Ellen almost under house arrest. But she was evidently a strong-willed girl with a mind of her own, for despite the strict surveillance she and Luke somehow managed to concoct a plot to outwit her father and unwelcome fiancé.

One day as Ellen walked out with a group of other well-bred girls, her only permitted companions and exercise, they stopped at a green area just inside the walls near the Peppergate. One of them suggested a ball game and the girls, who were in league with Ellen, played happily for a time until someone threw the

ball particularly high and it went over the wall into the street beyond. Ellen volunteered to fetch it, and screened by her friends slipped through the gate to Luke, who was waiting with two fast horses.

Ellen mounted, and the couple spurred their horses down Souters Lane towards the river. Crossing the Old Dee Bridge they headed for the young man's home in Wales, where among the wild terrain pursuit and discovery would be almost impossible. Back in Chester the girls waited a considerable time before they raised the alarm to give the pair sufficient opportunity for their escape.

When Ellen's flight was discovered her father was incensed. Unable to punish his daughter and her lover, he took out his spite on the innocent populace by ordering that the Peppergate be open to pedestrians only during the day, and closed completely each evening. This caused great inconvenience to townsfolk, who had to curtail visits to friends and markets outside Chester, and to tradesmen working in the city but living outside. It was a mean and unnecessary action which gave rise to a popular local saying of the day:

> 'When the daughter is stolen
> Shut the Peppergate.'

This having the same meaning as the more widely known 'Shutting the stable door after the horse has bolted'.

The story had a happy ending however. After their marriage in Wales, the couple went abroad and Luke prospered, distinguishing himself fighting in the Queen's service and this successful career resulted in Luke receiving a knighthood from Elizabeth. Luke and Ellen eventually returned to Chester as Lord and Lady Lacey, and were at long last reconciled with Ellen's father.

Chester's Ancient
Mystery Plays

Since its 10th century foundation men have lived out quiet uneventful lives behind the mighty walls of what was once St Werburgh's Abbey and is now Chester's ancient cathedral. Few of these mostly anonymous servants of God have managed to make a lasting impression on history, but at least two have left a literary legacy that can still be enjoyed today.

Although the original text is lost, the famous Chester Mystery Plays are believed to be the work of Ranulph Higden, a Benedictine monk who entered the Abbey in 1299. A noted historian and author, Higden certainly did write a seven volume work entitled *The Polychronicon*, an historical and geographical account of the world as he knew it, completed about 1350.

The title 'Mystery' is somewhat misleading; it does not refer to a medieval who-dun-it but to the fact that the performers were the working people of the city – the members of the trade guilds or 'mysteries' as they were alternatively known. These plays are believed to have been first staged in the 1320s, which would make them the oldest cycle of English religious dramas, predating those of York, Beverley and Coventry.

In an age when most ordinary people were illiterate the plays brought religion to the masses in a way they could understand and enjoy. It was drama written for the people and performed by them on the city streets. The participants took their parts very seriously; they could be fined for failing to turn up for a performance, or even forgetting a line.

Ranulph Higden, allied his obvious scholarship with a strong sense of humour. The dramas, although they have an underlying moral message, are extremely amusing, sometimes even to the point of bawdiness. The often outrageous characters like the cheating Ale-Wife in the *Hallowing of Hell*, and Noah's gossiping spouse who refuses to enter the Ark, were loved by all who came out in force to see them. They booed and hissed such arch-villains as the devil and King Herod, who were portrayed as comic figures. The personification of Jesus was always treated with true reverence.

The performances took place from the top of two-tier wagons that were towed about the city. The first would emerge from the Abbey gate, and after the show had taken place, move off to the High Cross where the drama was repeated. Meanwhile the second play would begin back at the Abbey, and the carts then proceeded in this manner around the town, making it possible for the townspeople to see the entire show from one spot. The upper part of the wagon acted as a stage, while the lower curtained section served as a dressing-room and storage place for props.

There were 26 plays in performance by 1467, telling biblical stories from the *Fall of Lucifer* to the *Last Judgement.* It is most unlikely that all of them could have been written by Ranulph. Probably more were added over the years, and the other monastic author is believed to have been another brother, Henry Francis.

The play was often appropriate to the guild that performed it. The *Flood* for instance being the property of the 'Water-drawers' of the Dee, and the *Sacrifice of Isaac* that of the barbers, presumably because of the knife that was to be used in the intended sacrifice! It appears that wives and children also took part, and were rewarded for doing so. In the reign of Elizabeth I, it is reported that one shilling was paid for the services of 'the infant Jesus', while 'Mary' received tenpence.

Originally the Mystery Plays delighted their audience at the feast of Corpus Christi (which varies between 23rd May and

33

24th June), but by 1521 they were taking place at Whitsun. Because of its length the entire cycle was performed over a three-day period, bringing the city to a complete standstill.

The performances were presented each year until 1535, by which time Puritanism was beginning to gain ground in the country. After the Reformation, although the plays had all direct references to the 'old religion' removed, their days were numbered.

Shows still took place intermittently until 1575, when the Archbishop of York announced a total ban. The ex-mayor Sir John Savage and his predecessor, John Hankey, were summoned to explain why they allowed the 'Popish plays of Chester', to take place. In their defence they pointed out that they were only carrying out the city council's instructions, and produced the minutes to prove it.

It would be interesting to know what Ranulph Higden and Henry Francis would have thought of this condemnation of their work. Brother Higden had sought what was considered in his time as the highest authority, having visited Rome to gain the permission of the Pope to stage the plays, but after the Reformation that authority was no longer accepted. The two monks would probably have appreciated the fact that thanks to copies made from medieval manuscripts in Elizabeth I's reign the dramas still live, and are performed to an enthusiastic audience once every five years on the Cathedral green.

The Belts of Congleton Wakes

In the not so distant past when leisure was a much prized commodity because it was so rare, the folk of Cheshire looked forward eagerly to their annual Wakes celebration. At one time a day of religious observance – when people watched or 'waked' in church on the eve of the local saint's day – this ritual later became purely an excuse for a day off work and having fun.

Congleton was no exception, but here, in addition to the side-shows, trinket-sellers, roundabouts and gypsy fortune-tellers, an age-old custom was observed each year. Before Henry VIII changed the nation's religion, at midnight on the eve of 12th August three monks would run through the streets of the town wearing over their shoulders broad leather belts with loose clappered bells, five on one and seven on both the others. It is said they made an extremely loud noise at the slightest movement.

The reason for this odd ritual was that the parish church had been dedicated to St Peter-ad-Vincula (St Peter in Chains), and the sound of the bells was meant to represent the captive apostle's chains on this, the eve of his feast day. When they heard the call, the local populace was required to assemble at the Town Cross to hear a sermon and to pray. It is doubtful that they welcomed this interruption to their night's sleep, so necessary to fortify them for the next day's festivities.

After the Reformation the religious aspect vanished, but the practice remained, the bells now becoming a symbol of the forthcoming Wakes. In Elizabeth I's reign the belts themselves passed out of the hands of the Church to the new custodians, a local family called Stubbes. When they first received this honour they were rich and powerful, the head of the clan being William Stubbes, a Queen's bailiff, and mayor of the town. However, by the 19th century their wealth had disappeared and they now followed the trade of chimney sweeps.

The senior members of the family nevertheless retained their ancient rights to parade the belts around the town each year. This they did with great enthusiasm throughout the day and night of 11th August, collecting a rowdy drunken mob which followed them to the Town Cross. On the way, all the while encouraging others to join in, they damaged property both accidently and by acts of deliberate vandalism, causing many complaints from the shopkeepers and business people of Congleton.

Around the mid-century the Stubbes family had a serious falling out, and two rival branches claimed ownership rights to the belts. This led to trouble as people took sides, and fights broke out between the two groups as they brawled through the streets, breaking windows and using as weapons whatever they could lay their hands on. Innocent bystanders were set upon, and people were put in fear of their lives. The business community really had cause for complaint now, as they had to put up their shutters for protection, losing valuable trade during Wakes Day. The sound of the bells no longer announced pleasures to come, but acted as a warning to clear the streets.

This situation continued for several years, until public pressure finally prevailed. While the people of Congleton were clearing up the mess after a particularly bad night of violence and mayhem, action was taken. The Town Clerk, John Wilson, went out with several burly constables to arrest the ringleaders while they were still suffering from the after effects of the previous night's excesses. They were thrown in gaol, and left there to contemplate their misdeeds.

After the rioters had endured a day and night of imprisonment, Wilson offered the heads of two rival 'fighting Stubbes' factions ten shillings each to give up 'all their claims, rights and titles and interests in the ancient chains of St Peter'. To this they agreed, tempted by what was then a generous sum of money.

The belts then disappeared into the civic archives, never again to act as the herald of Congleton Wakes.

The 'Bawming' Squires of Appleton Thorn

In 1178 Adam de Dutton, knight and landowner, returned to England after a period in the Holy Land fighting in the Crusades. To give thanks for his survival in the war against the Muslims, on the way home to Cheshire he made a pilgrimage to Glastonbury, where he acquired an offshoot of the Abbey's famous thorn bush.

The Glastonbury Thorn, renowned for flowering at Christmas time, is said to have grown from the staff of Joseph of Arimathaea, who donated his own tomb for the burial of Jesus. There is a legend that this Joseph was actually Christ's uncle, and that after the Crucifixion he journeyed to England and visited Glastonbury, bringing with him the Holy Grail, to house which he allegedly built the first English church.

The former crusader, ancestor of the Egerton-Warburton family, planted the cutting near his home at Arley. The village that grew up around Adam's tree took its name from this local landmark, becoming Appleton Thorn. The tree grew strong and tall, the centre of village life and also the focal point for the 'Bawming' ceremony that took place each year in late June.

'Bawming' is thought to come from an old dialect word meaning 'adorning', and involves the decorating of a tree. Following a parade through the village the young people of the area covered the branches with flags, red ribbons, and a wealth of fresh summer flowers. After this they danced around the tree, plaiting the ribbons in a similar fashion to the decking of a maypole. When the ceremony was completed there were games, races and a generous feast.

The origin of 'bawming' is somewhat obscure; it is believed to have its roots in ancient worship, where trees were thought to contain living spirits. Traces of old pagan religious practices survived long after the gods that they honoured were abandoned, so this could well be so.

Whatever the reason, the ceremonies continued for 800 years, until in the 1800s Adam de Dutton's tree, now aged and worn, fell victim to time. However, Rowland Eyles Egerton-Warburton, a descendant of the valiant crusader, now came to the rescue by providing a new tree. This was planted in 1888 in the grounds of his home, Arley Hall, by his daughter-in-law Mrs Piers Egerton-Warburton, to mark the occasion of her marriage.

Rowland, born in 1804 was known as the 'Rhyming Squire of Arley' and was famed for his rather bad poetry. As he was a keen horse-breeder and huntsman, much of his verse was dedicated to his favourite pastimes. In 1846 Rowland published a book entitled *Hunting Songs*, mainly for his friends in the Tarporley Hunt Club, but it proved so popular that it ran to eight editions in his lifetime.

Mr Egerton-Warburton had long been a supporter of the 'Bawming' ceremony even before his donation of a new tree. In 1870 he wrote the 'Bawming Song' which children have sung ever since while performing their dance, to the tune of 'Bonnie Dundee'.

> Up with fresh garlands this midsummer morn,
> Up with red ribbons on Appleton Thorn,
> Come lasses and lads to the Thorn Tree today,
> To bawm it and shout as ye bawm it 'hurray'.

After the death of Rowland in 1891 the ceremony lost its main sponsor, and the 'Bawmings' were suspended. There had been some rowdiness caused by people coming from nearby Warrington and even as far away as Manchester. Since the 18th century the occasion had become a very popular day out for big city dwellers, some of whom combined the celebration with bouts of over-indulgence in the local ales. Unfortunately such disruptions of the rural calm were increasing, and ended for a time an attractive local tradition.

In 1933 the ceremony was briefly revived only to lapse again. In 1965 the Egerton tree was blown down in a tremendous gale, and two years later another Glastonbury cutting was obtained, renewing interest in the ceremony. The new tree was placed near the church behind iron railings to protect it from modern vandals, and the 'Bawmings' were revived in 1973. Appleton Thorn is thought to be the only place in this country where the ancient rite is still observed.

The Marbury Dunne

Here lie the bones of the Marbury Dunne,
The finest Mare that ever run,
Clothed in a linen sheet,
With silver hooves upon her feet.

The Marbury Dunne rode into legend after an epic journey which was compared with the marathon feat performed between London and York by Dick Turpin's trusty Black Bess.

Lord Barrymore of Marbury Hall in the parish of Great Budworth was a wild young man who was both handsome and popular. He was also an inveterate gambler, a familiar figure at London gambling clubs and numerous private card parties, never known to miss an opportunity to place a bet or enjoy a novel wager with his friends.

Eventually, when a bride from a wealthy London family was selected for him the young noble was persuaded to marry and settle down. Lord Barrymore was not displeased when he saw the lady, for she was extremely beautiful. So happy was he with his prospective bride that he promised that whatever she most desired should be hers as a wedding gift.

The lady chose a fine horse that she knew was for sale. This was a greyish-brown thoroughbred, known as the Dunne Mare. Lord Barrymore purchased the horse and told his future wife that the animal would arrive at Marbury Hall on her wedding day. While the bride travelled north to prepare for her marriage Barrymore decided to stay in the capital enjoying his last few weeks as a bachelor.

During this time, while playing cards with a group of

friends Lord Barrymore regaled them with descriptions of the horse he had bought for his bride. He praised the beauty, and boasted of the prowess of the animal, and as the night progressed with the wine flowing freely, the claims became more and more extravagant. This led eventually to the bridegroom betting that his wedding gift could leave London at sunrise and arrive at Marbury in time to greet his guests at sunset.

On the morning of the marriage the horse set off from London ridden by an amateur jockey, cheered on by a crowd of well-wishers. Meanwhile back in Cheshire the wedding took place, followed by a lavish reception, and as the pleasant summer evening drew to a close the company assembled in the courtyard to await the Dunne. Some doubted that the animal could complete the run in time and mentally counted their winnings, while the Dunne's backers scanned the horizon together with the anxious Lady Barrymore.

At last, just before the sun set, a dust cloud appeared in the distance and the pound of those famed silver-shod hooves could be distinctly heard. Soon the Marbury Dunne galloped through the gates into the courtyard, lathered with sweat and blood mingling with the foam on her muzzle. Despite this, she still presented an impressive sight; a finer horse, as the rhyme states, had never been seen locally.

The exhausted jockey now led his mount to a well at the centre of the yard, but as she tried to drink the gallant animal collapsed and died, her poor heart having failed after her terrible exertion. Weeping hysterically the distraught Lady Barrymore had to be led from the distressing scene.

The Dunne was buried in the grounds of the 13th century hall and the above verse was inscribed on the gravestone. Its young mistress was heartbroken, and from the day of her marriage she pined for her horse, refusing all food. As the days and weeks passed, gradually she became weaker. It was said she died of grief; though not actively supporting the bet, she blamed herself for doing nothing to prevent it.

The lady made a dying request that she be buried beside

the well at the very spot her beloved horse had died. To humour her Lord Barrymore pretended to agree, but later, fearing public outrage, had his wife buried more conventionally in the churchyard.

Three days after the funeral Lord Barrymore returned home to find his wife waiting for him beside the well. Her ghostly form told him that because he had denied her dying wish, she could not rest peacefully. As his punishment, for the remainder of his life at Marbury, each night at dusk her husband had to endure the sight of his lady riding her adored Dunne Mare.

The Saxon Crosses of Sandbach

In the market square of Sandbach are two stone pillars, one 16 ft high, the other smaller at ten ft nine ins. These structures are merely shafts of the original Saxon crosses that marked the arrival of Christianity in the area.

The age of the crosses is disputed, but they are generally thought to have been erected by Peada, a 7th century king of Mercia who ruled an area which included present day Cheshire. In AD 653 this pagan monarch fell in love with Alchfleda, the beautiful daughter of King Oswi of Northumbria. The princess's father had just been converted to the Christian religion, and would not hear of a non-believer paying court to his only daughter. Peada, desperate to wed his love, promised that if he were given permission to marry he would become a Christian.

The couple's wedding took place in the lady's kingdom, and the bride and groom then travelled back to Mercia in state, at the head of a large army. Once home again Peada, true to his word became a Christian, and with the zeal of a convert ruled that all his subjects must follow his example. To mark his recent baptism and show commitment to his new faith the king ordered the erection of the mighty crosses.

Peada threw himself wholeheartedly into his new religion, and chose Sandbach as an important religious centre for Mercia. It is thought the presence of the crosses there point to the existence of an influential Christian building outside which they stood, and from where missionaries were sent to convert the rest of the country.

It is still possible to make out some of the carving on the pillars. The larger of the two has vine scrolls and animals in the branches of trees, symbols of Alchfleda's Northumbrian home. There are also religious figures still discernible on the south side of the shaft: Christ on the Cross, a Nativity scene, the four Evangelists, an angel, also a lion, calf and eagle. In addition, there are figures on a ladder that some experts believe could represent the descent of the Holy Spirit, or alternatively that the men could be the Mercian warriors who accompanied Peada to claim his bride. They travelled as fighting men, carrying various weapons, and returned after their conversion – having taken the biblical advice to turn their swords into ploughshares – bearing only wooden staffs.

As time passed Mercia's king may have wondered if he had made the right decision in becoming a man of peace, for he discovered that his adored Christian wife had plotted with disaffected elements in the realm to have him assassinated. Possibly she had become bored and disillusioned with her pious husband, and craved the excitement of ruling in his stead. Peada had the ring-leaders put to death, but true to his new beliefs forgave Alchfleda, though no doubt keeping a wary eye on her in the future.

The crosses, Peada's lasting memorial, are unusual in that they have more in common with the Celtic monuments found in Scotland and Ireland than anything seen in England. How they would have looked in their heyday can only now be imagined, as they suffered damage at the time of the Reformation and again during the Civil War when Oliver Cromwell's men also took exception to these religious relics, smashing them completely. The remnants of Sandbach's Saxon past disappeared for close on 150 years, during which time the fragments were put to many different uses, including garden ornaments, serving as paving stones and even providing a cottage step.

Then in 1816 Sir John Egerton of Oulton Park offered to relinquish the two large sections that were built into a grotto in his grounds. Subscriptions were collected to fund the tracing and return of all fragments and the reassembly of the crosses. The historian George Ormerod and the architect John Palmer collected all the parts that could be traced and lovingly pieced them together, siting the monuments in their present position.

The pillars still stand proudly in the centre of the town, reminders of a long ago royal romance with a not so happy ending.

The Horned Woman
of Saughall

Saughall is a quiet, pleasant village a couple of miles outside the city of Chester with few claims to international recognition. It did however have a resident who gained fame – if not fortune – in the 17th century.

Mary Davies was born in nearby Shotwick in 1600, and after an unremarkable girlhood married a Saughall man. The match was a good one, as her husband Henry was a farmer who possessed a holding of £16 per annum under the Crown.

They settled down to a comfortable married life until, at the age of 28, Mary developed a lump on either side of her head. The couple sought medical advice, but the doctors were baffled. The young woman appeared otherwise to be in excellent health, with no further symptoms apart from her distressing deformity. The best explanation that the medical science of the day could come up with was that the problem had been caused by wearing a tight hat for too long a period. However, although the bumps remained, as Mary was fit and no other problems occurred she accepted her lot and got on with life.

In 1641 her husband died and Mary, unable to stay on the farm, was now forced to find another way of earning her living. She duly became a midwife, and moved into a small cottage in the village, which still stands at the side of the present day Vernon Institute.

When Mary reached her late fifties and was still actively pursuing her profession, the mysterious lumps suddenly changed character. The poor woman now developed two horns that were solid and wrinkled, rising to a point about one and a half inches behind and above her ears. They then curved downwards towards the back of her neck, similar in nature to those of a ram. Distressing though these appendages must have been, the horns it seems proved quite useful as a barometer, as it was said that they 'sadly grieved her upon a change in the weather'.

After five years she shed her strange projections only to grow two more that lasted a further four years, when Mary again cast her horns and grew another pair. These proved to be her last, surviving until Mary's death in her early seventies, by which time they were beginning to loosen.

During this period the unfortunate woman must have been an object of great curiosity, for even though her neighbours became used to her appearance, many outsiders flocked to Saughall to catch a glimpse. The horns became prized items; a nobleman obtained a pair Mary had shed and presented them to the king of France, who evidently was intrigued by the phenomenon. Mary also travelled to London where she was exhibited at the Swan Inn, near Charing Cross, and it was here that the sight of her inspired a local ballad writer to pen the following verse:

> 'Ye that love wonders to behold,
> Here you may of a wonder read,
> The strangest that was ever seen or told,
> A woman with horns upon her head.'

In 1668 a portrait was commissioned of Mary aged 68, which was displayed in the Ashmolean Museum in Oxford for some years, together with a pair of her horns, although no trace of them exists today. However, a small likeness does hang in the Vernon Institute close to her old home.

No answer was ever found as to why Mary Davies was afflicted in this way. Numerous physicians examined her, but none could put forward anything other than their personal theories. It does appear though that the horns were accepted as genuine and were not an elaborate confidence trick. Indeed apart from her trip to London Mary made little money from her celebrity status. Deception or not, no one succeeded in disproving the authenticity of the 'Horned Woman of Saughall'.

Emma, the Blacksmith's Daughter

When she was born on 26th April 1761 at Swan Cottage in the Wirral village of Ness, no one could have foreseen what the future held for little Amy Lyon. The entry into the world of this child of Henry Lyon, the village blacksmith and his wife Mary, a former domestic servant, must surely have passed almost unnoticed.

Amy was soon to leave the area, for tragedy struck when Henry died shortly after her birth, and Mary returned with her baby to her native Hawarden just over the border in North Wales. Here, they suffered considerable poverty without a male provider, and during Amy's childhood they were forced to earn a living selling coal from baskets strapped to a donkey.

As Amy, or 'Emy' as she now liked to be called, grew older it became obvious she was destined to be a great beauty. There was a slight flaw to her appearance though, she sometimes suffered from an unsightly skin condition. In 1778, 17 year old Emy travelled back to Cheshire in an attempt to seek a remedy. Situated on the Dee, Parkgate was rapidly gaining a reputation for beneficial sea-bathing, also for a treatment involving seaweed and salt water that was said to aid such problems as Emy's. It seemed to work for her, because she wrote to a friend 'My knees is well . . . there is hardly a mark, and my elbows is much better. If I stay a fortnight longer I will not have a spot, for you can scarce discover anything on my knees and arms.'

Emy stayed at a house on the front during her visit, and

spent a pleasant summer in the up-and-coming resort near to her birth-place before going to London to seek her fortune. Once there she began work as a nursemaid, but the vivacious, lovely girl found this occupation rather tame for her liking. Now a talented amateur actress and singer, she sought more exciting and better paid employment entertaining at gambling clubs and private functions. It was at this time also that she changed her name to the more fashionable Emma. She formed various attachments, from which she had two children.

While engaged in entertaining she met the handsome, dashing Sir Charles Greville, a charming man, but also a compulsive gambler. In 1782 Emma became his mistress, enabling her to move freely in London society and to improve her knowledge of music and develop an interest in literature. Emma captivated all who met her, and great artists were inspired to portray her beauty on canvas. Romney is said to have painted her 23 times, and she also sat for Sir Joshua Reynolds.

When she was 25 pressing debts forced Emma and Charles to flee to Naples, where Charles's uncle, Sir William Hamilton, was ambassador to what was then an independent kingdom. Greville hoped to persuade his relative to assist him financially, but elderly Sir William fell deeply in love with Emma on sight, and Charles virtually sold her to his uncle in return for the settlement of his debts. Four years later the couple returned to England, and in 1791 Emma and Sir William were married in St Marylebone church, London.

Emma was now among the most famous beauties of her time, intelligent and witty. She was also described as impulsive, courageous, and alternating between violent rages and tenderness. On their return to Naples the ambassador and his wife continued their close friendship with King Ferdinand and Queen Maria Carolina. There, in 1793, she first met the man who was to become the great love of her life, Horatio Nelson; it is said that on their first encounter she fainted in his arms. Nelson continued his victorious career, losing an eye at Calvi in 1794 and his right arm in 1796 at

Santa Cruz. In 1798 came his massive defeat of the French fleet off Aboukir Bay, known as the Battle of the Nile. He returned to Naples to a hero's welcome, especially from Emma Hamilton, who became his mistress about this time. Now in her late thirties and still a lovely woman, Emma had used her considerable influence to negotiate a safe haven for the British fleet after the Battle of the Nile.

Nelson remained at the Court of Naples, where he and Emma were able to enjoy a blissful period until, threatened by the French, they assisted the royal family's flight to the safety of Sicily. In 1800, once back in England, Nelson settled into the Hamilton's home as a permanent guest, having now separated from his wife. Sir William seemed to accept his wife's liaison, and remained on good terms with the couple until his death in 1803.

In 1801 the daughter of Emma and Nelson, Horatia, was born in secrecy while her father was away at sea. They also had a second girl, who sadly died in infancy. After the death of Sir William, Emma moved into Nelson's home in Merton.

Nelson regarded Emma as his 'guardian angel' and kept a miniature of her in his cabin at all times. In October 1805, on the eve of his death at Trafalgar, he left an unfinished letter which began 'My dearest beloved Emma, the dear friend of my bosom, the signal has been made that the enemy's combined fleet are coming out of port . . .

Despite a codicil to Nelson's will bequeathing Emma and Horatia to the nation on the grounds that the former had rendered important service to the state, financial recognition was denied. Nelson had left Emma his Merton home, £2,000 and an annuity of £150, but through her gambling, drinking and other extravagances within a few years she and her daughter were reduced to poverty.

In 1813 the once beautiful Emma spent 12 months in prison for debt, and after being released on bail she escaped with her daughter to Calais. It was here in 1815, far from her Cheshire roots, that Amy Lyon, the blacksmith's daughter, died in obscurity.

The Regicide of Marple Hall

A fter having been the property of the noble Stanleys, early in the 17th century, historic Marple Hall became the home of the Bradshaw family, and it was here that the three sons of Henry Bradshaw grew up. The entry in the register of Stockport Parish Church records that on 10th December 1602 John, the third boy, was baptised. Against this entry someone later added the solitary word, 'Traitor'.

It appears that the young John had some form of premonition that he would one day perform a momentous act, for while he was a pupil at King Edward's Grammar School in Macclesfield he wrote the following on a grave-stone:

> My brother Harry must heir the land,
> My brother Frank must be at his command,
> While I, poor Jack must do that,
> Which all the world will wonder at.

On leaving school John Bradshaw became a lawyer's clerk at Congleton and, deciding this was the career he wanted to follow, went to London to study at Gray's Inn. In 1627, at the age of 25 he was called to the bar, and later returned to Congleton as a councillor-at-law and a councillor to the corporation. In 1637 he served as the town's mayor, and that same year became Attorney General for Cheshire and Flintshire, then despite having lived in London for three years on 22 February 1646 he was appointed Chief Justice of Chester.

A staunch republican whose sympathies were with the Parliamentarian cause during England's Civil War, in 1644 John was engaged by Parliament to prosecute two Irish lords, McMahon and Maguire. It was as prosecutor that he achieved notoriety several years later.

In 1649 John Bradshaw was chosen – it is said against his will – to be President of the Commission to try the defeated and imprisoned King Charles I. Despite his alleged reluctance Bradshaw did however make a 'large speech', about what he called 'the King's misgovernment'. This was not likely to make him popular in all quarters, and as he walked through the streets to the court each day in his distinctive scarlet robes, he also wore a beaver hat lined with steel, and was flanked by a large number of bodyguards.

The king was duly convicted, and the first of the 58 signatures on Charles' execution warrant was that of John Bradshaw. It seems he had no regrets, for as he stated afterwards, 'Had it to be done again, I would be the first man in England to do it'. However, despite his strong beliefs in the Parliamentary system of government, John Bradshaw was not afraid to speak out when he thought Oliver Cromwell had overstepped his authority. When in 1655 the Lord Protector dismissed the Council and dissolved Parliament, Bradshaw told him: 'Sir we have heard what you did at the House this morning and before many hours all England will know it, but Sir, you are mistaken to think that Parliament is dissolved, no power under heaven can dissolve them but themselves.'

Shortly after his courageous stand Bradshaw contracted the plague and in 1659 died from this terrible disease. His critics not surprisingly claimed this to be his punishment for what they considered to be the crime of regicide, the murder of an anointed monarch.

Despite their differences Cromwell accorded Justice Bradshaw honour in death; he received the distinction of burial in Westminster Abbey among the nation's greatest figures. He was not destined to enjoy a peaceful rest; when

Charles II was restored in 1660 many old scores were settled. John Bradshaw's bones were dug up and ceremonially hanged at Tyburn, the fate of a regicide that many would have liked to inflict on the living man.

After Bradshaw's death a ghost was said to have begun haunting his old home at Marple. Some believed it to be that of Charles Stuart come to torment the family of his accuser. Another legend has it that the spirit was of a Royalist officer who loved the niece of John Bradshaw. His elder brother Henry, also a dedicated Parliamentarian discovered that the young man had secretly visited his daughter at the Hall and ordered a servant to follow and kill him. This the man did, throwing the body into the nearby river Goyt.

Whoever the spirit was that haunted Marple Hall, both contenders had died tragically and violently at the hands of their fellow men. For this reason the ghost was referred to as the 'Martyr'.

The Noble Grosvenors

When William the Conqueror defeated King Harold in 1066 he gained with his new kingdom much desirable land, some of which he then distributed amongst his favourites. As would be expected his nephew Hugh of Avaranche received his share; William accorded the Earldom of Chester and all the estate and wealth that it possessed to his relative.

Norman Hugh soon found out that he would have to fight to retain his property as Chester was a stronghold of support for the Saxon cause, and the Welsh also proved a constant threat. So ruthlessly did Hugh deal with all opposition that he gained the nickname 'Lupus', Latin for wolf.

In addition to fighting Hugh Lupus liberally enjoyed food, wine and women; according to a contemporary report he was 'much given to his belly', and he also fathered more than 20 illegitimate children. However, the greatest passion in his life was undoubtedly hunting, and it was this that gained the family its surname. As well as 'Lupus', Hugh had earned the title 'Gros Veneur' (Grosvenor), which in Norman-French means 'great hunter'. The 'Gros' does also mean fat, and some less than generous people have suggested this was what had been intended. Hugh would certainly have qualified for either as he weighed 20 stone, and towards the end of his life the only way he could ride was to be hoisted with a block and tackle on to a mighty shire horse.

Because of the debauched life he had led the earl as he grew older began to fear for his immortal soul. Particularly in his younger days Hugh Lupus had shown less than due reverence for the Church, and on one occasion had kennelled his hounds in a church overnight. A lesson should

58

have been learned from this, for the following day all the dogs were found dead. In 1093 Hugh repented, and fearing the impending judgment of his maker he founded the Benedictine Abbey of St Werburgh, where the monks were to spend their lives in solemn prayer for the soul of their patron. The earl lived a further eight years, dying in 1101.

If legend is to be believed, the actions Hugh took in his life continued to affect his family long after his death. The Earl had cruelly tortured and killed a young gypsy boy he caught poaching on his land, and the lad's family pronounced a curse on the Grosvenors, that no son would follow father in the succession to the earldom. Hugh's only legitimate heir did succeed, but only to die without heirs in the so-called 'White Ship' disaster of 1120. William, the only son of Henry I had travelled to France to claim his bride when on the return journey his vessel sank in the English Channel, drowning the prince and many other members of the nobility. The 'Grosvenor Curse' as it became known has cropped up in later generations also, the 2nd, 3rd, 4th and 5th dukedoms passed to cousins.

After Hugh Lupus, the family no longer played such a prominent part in the country's affairs until the 'Great Dispute' of 1385. The Grosvenors had adopted as their emblem a diagonal gold bar on a blue shield, or in heraldry terms, the 'Bend Or'. When Sir Robert Grosvenor accompanied Richard II to fight against the Scots, it was noted his crest was the same as that of Lord Scrope of Bolton, an important courtier and former holder of such high offices as Treasurer and Chancellor of England.

Lord Scrope was extremely annoyed to find an almost unknown knight carrying the same crest as himself, and the argument which arose was referred to the Court of Chivalry. Such influential men as John of Gaunt and his son Henry Bolingbroke (later Henry IV) and even Geoffrey Chaucer gave evidence in Scrope's favour, and the Grosvenors lost the case. They then substituted the 'Garb Or' or Cheshire sheaf for the 'Bend Or'.

The family may have lost its favoured emblem, but it increased its wealth over the years by prudent marriages with rich heiresses. The most lucrative of these was the union of Sir Thomas Grosvenor in 1677 with 12 year old Mary Davies of Ebury in Middlesex. Mary's father, Alexander Davies, was a lawyer who had inherited estates from a rich uncle, Hugh Audley. Davies had also 'acquired' other properties in London by retaining the deeds which the owners had lodged with him before their flight from the Plague and the Great Fire of 1665-6. They did not return to claim their properties – perhaps because they had perished in one of the disasters. Whatever the reason lawyer Davies took possession of their estates, so that with his legitimate inheritance he owned properties which included Westminster, Victoria, Mayfair and Belgravia, prime areas of real estate today. All those the Grosvenors received as Mary's dowry.

The family became rich and powerful, receiving a dukedom in 1874, but they did not forget their former coat of arms. The 1st Duke called his favourite race-horse, which won the 1880 Derby, 'Bend Or'. The 2nd Duke, a leading socialite in the early years of the 20th century was also nicknamed 'Bend Or' after his grandfather's horse. In 1909 the five year old son of 'Bend Or' died from appendicitis and it seemed that the 'Curse of the Grosvenors' had struck again, for despite marrying four times, the second Duke never produced another heir. However, as the present 6th Duke whose home is at Eaton Hall, near Chester did succeed his father, it may be that the crime of Hugh Lupus has at last been expiated.

Shakespeare's Dark Lady

There is no record of William Shakespeare having visited Cheshire, but it is possible that he was inspired to write some of his most powerful sonnets by a dark beauty of the county, for belief exists that Mary, the lovely daughter of Sir Edward Fitton of Gawsworth Hall, is the mysterious 'Dark Lady', of Shakespeare's sonnets 127–152.

The family background of this country gentlewoman was impeccable. Sir Edward, born in 1550, was a distinguished man who, after being knighted at the age of 30, spent some years in the prestigious position of Lord President of Munster. His marriage to Alice Holcroft produced four children, two sons, Edward and Richard, and daughters Anne, born 1574, and Mary in 1578.

It seems rather appropriate that Mary was baptised on 24th June for it seems a strain of midsummer madness ran through her eventful life.

As the two girls grew up in rural Gawsworth it became apparent Mary would be the more attractive and charismatic of the pair. Anne did make a good match when she wed Sir John Newdigate, but it was Mary who was chosen for a life at court. Queen Elizabeth I in her declining years loved to be surrounded by beautiful young women, they perhaps brought back the more pleasant memories of her own turbulent and often perilous youth. Whatever the reason, in 1596 she readily accepted the 17 year old Mary Fitton as a maid of honour.

The proud parents saw this as a considerable advancement for their younger daughter, particularly as she soon became a favourite of the queen. Sir Edward and Lady Alice no doubt expected that the royal maids of the 'Virgin Queen' would be

cared for and strictly supervised. This does not appear to have been the case. A leading courtier, Sir Francis Knollys, who was lodged near to the maids' dormitory complained bitterly about the girls' conduct declaring their 'frisking about' caused him 'extreme disquiet'.

If he had realised the extent of Mary's activities, Knollys would have been even more concerned. At night, disguised as a man she would steal away from court to meet her lovers at disreputable city taverns. These men who engaged private rooms in which to entertain her were influential figures of the day. They included William Herbert, poet and later the 3rd Earl of Pembroke, Sir Richard Leveson, a notable seafarer and vice-admiral of England, and also William Shakespeare.

Mary was lively and popular, she also had a flair for drama and enjoyed taking part in theatricals. In June 1600, at a musical entertainment performed in the queen's honour, Mary played the leading part. She again indulged her love of dressing up; it was reported she wore a skirt of cloth of silver and a waistcoat 'wrought with silkes and gold', her lovely dark hair – so admired by Shakespeare, who called her 'Black beauty's successive heir' – was said to have 'hung loose about her shoulders'.

It is likely that Mary Fitton met Shakespeare through her interest in the stage. By the time she arrived at court he was an actor with, and the regular playwright to the Lord Chamberlain's Men. If Mary was indeed the Dark Lady, she and Shakespeare formed a liaison which does not seem to have been a very happy one. In many of the sonnets devoted to the Dark Lady the poet accuses his love of faithlessness, and comments adversely on her behaviour.

The probability of Mary being Shakespeare's 'Dark Lady' might well be borne out by her relationship with William Herbert. Some scholars are of the opinion that he is the 'Mr W. H' to whom the first 127 sonnets are dedicated ('the onlie begetter'). In several of the 'Dark Lady' sonnets Shakespeare rails at her for alienating the affections of his friend; in fact one hints at a double betrayal: the friend with the mistress and the mistress with the friend:

> Isn't not enough to torture me alone,
> But slave to slavery my sweet'st friend must be?
> Me from myself thy cruel eye hath taken,
> And my next self thou harder hast engross'd,
> Of him, myself, and thee I am forsaken,
> A torment thrice threefold thus to be cross'd.

Throughout these later sonnets runs the thread of disillusionment and betrayal, seeming to suggest that William Herbert, one of Mary Fitton's lovers and therefore Shakespeare's rival, was the 'sweet'st friend' alluded to, and Mary Fitton the Dark Lady.

Shakespeare also writes of her false beauty:

> Sweet beauty hath no name, no holy bower,
> But is profaned, if not lives in disgrace.

This disgrace became apparent in 1602, when Mary became pregnant, reputedly by William Herbert. The future earl was Elizabeth's godson, and she was incensed by the behaviour of these two young people whom she loved and trusted. Herbert, when challenged, admitted the affair, but refused to marry Mary owing to her continuing relationships with other men; he named one rival not as Shakespeare but as Richard Leveson. Was this because an actor-playwright was not worthy of mention, or because of his friendship with Shakespeare? The queen was extremely angry at what she saw as a scandalous situation and declared that 'both would do well in the tower awhile'. William Herbert was indeed jailed, but only for a short time; he was soon released, fined and banished to his Wiltshire estates. Mary herself was sent from court also, and returned to Gawsworth where her child, a son, was stillborn.

The Fittons were devastated; in their family such disgrace had never occurred before. Lady Alice wrote to her other daughter, Anne, 'I take no joy to hear of your sister'. She continues 'I would sooner be buried and see her the same, than suffer the great deal of shame as never have a Cheshire woman borne.'

The following year the queen died, and King James of Scotland came to the throne. This was fortunate for Mary; her brother Edward was popular with the new monarch, and so able to secure his sister's return to court. She had not learnt her lesson however, and soon resumed her affair with Richard Leveson, by whom she had two illegitimate daughters.

The family must have been very relieved when in 1606 Mary finally married a Captain William Polwhele, who no doubt had needed some financial persuasion to accept a bride with such a tarnished reputation. The union was short lived as Polwhele died in 1610; however, his widow, who had now settled down to domestic respectability, soon found another husband. This second marriage to Captain John Lougher lasted longer, his death not occurring until 1635. Mary herself lived to witness the turmoil of England's Civil War, finally dying in 1647.

It is not certain where Mary Fitton was laid to rest. A move to dig up the floor of Gawsworth church last century to see if she was interred there was thankfully prevented. Mary Fitton's effigy does appear though, kneeling at the feet of her parents' tomb in St James's church. The demure little figure belies the colourful life led by this reckless Cheshire beauty whose loveliness may have inspired England's greatest poet to immortalise in verse his adored but faithless 'Dark Lady'.

The Fire of Nantwich

A strong westerly wind whipped through the streets on that cold afternoon of Tuesday 10 December 1583. In Nantwich – with Middlewich and Northwich being the three 'wiches' famous for salt production – it was a day like any other. No citizen could have visualised the devastation that would be revealed by the next morning's light in a town described by William Smith three years previously as 'accorded the greatest town in Cheshire, next to Chester'.

In the High Street house belonging to John Crewe, but leased by Nicholas Brown, the evening meal was being prepared, a meal that was to have dreadful consequences for the people of Nantwich. At about 4 pm a fire broke out in the kitchen which could not be contained and it quickly spread to the wooden beams of the roof, blazed through the thatch and, aided by the strong wind, set alight first the adjoining premises then rapidly engulfed its neighbours.

As the fire raged through High Street, the local populace ran from their homes, combining in a desperate struggle to save their properties. The firefighting methods were primitive; water was brought in buckets from the river Weaver, and the men seized what ladders they could to reach the blazing roofs. 'Firehooks', long poles with hooks on the end, were also used to pull burning hatch to the ground, even mud and earth were used to douse the flames.

The women fought bravely alongside their menfolk, carrying from the river water in anything they could lay their hands on, forming a human chain as they passed the containers from one to another. Ann, wife of Thomas Lovatt, was killed doing just this, when the wall of Nicholas Brown's house fell on her.

The frantic operation was not helped by John Seckerston, the landlord of the Bear Inn. As the flames approached his premises Seckerston, fearing for their lives, released the four bears which gave his hostelry its name. The poor frightened creatures wandered about the town, so terrifying the fire-fighters that the women demanded armed guards.

The fire burned unabated, in the words of eye-witness, Richard Wilbraham, 'consuming all the buildings in the high town upon both sides, it then joined to the waterlode and up to Pillory Street'. All the houses in Pillory Street were destroyed, Wilbraham reports, 'except one belonging to Robert Goddier'. It devoured both sides of Hospital Street, stopping only at the 'home of Thomas Wright on the south side, and at the house of the Wilbrahams of Woodehey'. The blaze then ripped along Church Lane, passing the church-yard and sparing St Mary's, then continuing along Pepper Street and burning all premises in Beam Street and Love Lane. Wilbraham states 'and in this cruel fire there was left no manner of timber building, of any house in all these streets, except one piece of a wall of the house wherein it began.'

In the 15 hours the fire burned, 150 houses were destroyed, also numerous shops, kitchens, two horse mills, a barn, a stable and some pig sties in which the unfortunate animals also perished. Seven inns were lost: the Cock, Bell, Crown, Harts Horn, Swan, Ship and Mr Seckerston's Bear.

Considering the destruction of property, loss of life was comparatively light; apart from Ann Lovatt, only two other persons died, a young woman called Margery Duckworth, and an elderly widow, Alice Blagge, both unable to escape the conflagration. Richard Wilbraham felt the fire was a warning to the people of Nantwich to behave themselves, and that the saving of the church was to be seen as a mark of heavenly favour. The death toll would have been much higher but for the fact that the constables Thomas Minshull and his cousin Matthew Wright, had just moved 17 cart loads of ammunition out of the town the previous day.

By 8 am the following morning the battle was won, and

exhausted firefighters viewed the wreckage of their homes. The blaze had destroyed most of the town east of the river and many buildings still smouldered throughout the next few days, needing constant damping down. Wilbraham declares that for another 20 days fires could still be detected in the cellars of the affected area.

The townsfolk now counted their losses. A number of people living further from the seat of the fire did have time to save some of their household goods. Many had considerable losses however. Thomas Minshull, a mercer (perhaps the same man who had removed the explosives, for the role of constable was not full time), records losing from his Pepper Street house, 'panelling, bedsteads, stools, chairs, plate, a drinking can, four plain, and twelve apostle spoons, and a silver salt, worth £28!

The first priority when the shock had subsided was to plan for the rebuilding of the town. A fund was hurriedly launched to which the local gentry contributed generously. The Cholmondeleys, Mainwarings and Wilbrahams dug deep into their coffers. When the Dean of St Pauls, Alexander Newell, informed Elizabeth I of the tragedy, the queen diverted £1,000 from government funds, and authorised a nationwide collection. She also gave permission for wood from the royal forest of Delamere to be used for the rebuilding.

The new Nantwich rose like a phoenix from the ashes of its destruction, and the people did not forget the debt they owed the queen for her help in its reconstruction. A plaque placed on a house erected in High Street by master-carpenter Thomas Cleese can still be seen over the present-day shop, commemorating Elizabeth's part in the town's rebirth. It bears the following verse:

> 'God Grante Our Royal Queen,
> In England Longe to Reign
> For She Hath Put Her Helping Hand
> To Bild This Towne Again.'

'A Souling'

The traditional Souling Play was once a familiar part of country life throughout the land. In Cheshire, however, the custom had some unique differences.

This play was performed on or around All Souls' Day, 2nd November, the festival on which families fondly remembered their departed loved ones. Before the Reformation poor people would tour the district begging money to pay for masses to be said in memory of their relatives, but later this practice evolved into collecting for purely secular reasons. Groups would visit various houses locally, singing or performing in return for such rewards as small spiced 'soul cakes' or, better still, contributions of money.

These callers were not always welcome. Around the middle of the last century a master of hounds living near Chester was not at all amused when he was disturbed at his dinner by a party of 'Soulers'. So upset was the gentleman at this interruption that he seized his shotgun and fired, sending them running for their lives.

A better reception was accorded in most homes however, and the little drama that had as its central theme the triumph of good over evil was generally enjoyed by householders. In the Antrobus version, still performed by the Comerbach Mummers in local pubs, the hero is brave St George, who issues the challenge:

> 'I am the champion bold,
> And who is he who dares against me stand,
> I'll swear I'll cut him down with my
> Victorious brand.'

69

The hero then does battle with the evil villain 'Slasher', although in other versions this character's name can vary. In Tarvin the enemy was the 'Turkish Champion', possibly dating from the Crusades.

Following a furious mock sword fight, St George would strike down his foe. A comical figure, the quack doctor appeared, and after a recitation concerning his magic powers he would restore the slain man to life. Another humourous character was Beelzebub, a comic devil who could also be called 'Belcher Bob' in some places. These variations probably stem from the fact that the dialogue was never written down, having been passed through the generations by means of the spoken word. So it is easy to see how changes took place.

Souling continued to be generally popular right up to the outbreak of the Second World War. However, it was only in Cheshire that you would have found the addition called 'Hodening', or the introduction of the 'Wild Horse'.

In Sandiway the animal was called 'Dick' and was accompanied by his 'driver'. The 'horse' was actually a man dressed in a white sheet and with a head that contained snapping hinged jaws. In Antrobus the 'driver' is dressed as a huntsman who praises the animal's attributes before attempting to sell him to the audience. The 'horse' himself leaps around, mock-terrifying people by snapping his jaws at them.

'Hodening' is thought not to be a true feature of Souling, but just performed at the same time of year. It has even been suggested that the custom is derived from Norse mythology where in October horses were sacrificed to the god Odin. The word 'Hoden' could, of course, have come from Odin. In Comberbach though, the horse is said to represent the famous 'Dunne' mare who completed a record-breaking run from London to Marbury Hall.

The spectacle seems to have been quite an alarming experience. In Great Budworth and Higher Whitley a real horse's skull was used. Sandiway Dick's head was obtained from a local hunt kennel where the hounds had just eaten the flesh. At Higher Whitley's Hodening a ritual funeral service was held after the performance, when the skull would be buried. Here rival gangs of youths from nearby villages often attempted to steal the skull, and fights broke out for its possession. With red rings painted around the eyes the desired object was horrible to behold, a sight from which children fled in fear.

For the main part however, performers and spectators alike seemed to have had fun. Indeed towards the end of the last century the Sandiway 'Hodening' was criticised for being no better than an excuse for a 'boozy pub crawl'. The custom died out here in 1907, temperance having gained the upper hand.

Knutsford's
Danish Legacy

Though Mrs Gaskell put Knutsford on the literary map, it was an 11th century royal visit that gave the town its name, and also a unique custom that still survives.

In 1016, after his defeat by Canute, the newly elected English king Edmund 'Ironside' was forced to divide his kingdom with the Danish victor. But in November 1016, before the Ashington treaty could be implemented, Edmund died, leaving Canute undisputed ruler of all England. The following year, while marching through Mercia on the way north to fight the Scots, Canute and his army forded the Lily, a small river in what is now Cheshire. After his men had crossed the river, the king stopped to empty sand that had collected in his shoes. At this moment he saw a wedding party approaching. Canute wished the couple every happiness and after sprinkling the sand in their path he expressed a hope that the marriage would be blessed with as many children as the falling grains of sand.

Whether the young couple did have an enormous family is not known, but the incident had such a lasting effect on the memory of the local people that they named the place where the king chose to cross Cnuts Ford (Knutsford) in his honour. Legend has it that the other rather more amusing outcome of the meeting was the ritual of 'Sanding', a custom to be found nowhere else in the country.

The practice involves the design of pictures formed by trickling white sand through a funnel on to a groundwork of brown sand. In this way, attractive sketches and mottoes were created on the pavements of Knutsford outside the houses of couples about to wed. The designs included hearts, flowers, and lovers-knots, and sentiments such as

'Long may they live, and happy may they be,
Blest with content, and from misfortune free.'

On the morning of their marriage, on waking up, both bride and groom would find the sand pictures outside their doors, and the greeting might also have appeared at the homes of friends and neighbours. Mrs Elizabeth Gaskell herself experienced this charming custom before her wedding at Knutsford parish church on 30th August 1832.

As well as 'Sanding' delighting couples on their wedding day it also welcomed visiting dignitaries. While still a young princess, Victoria was said to have been 'surprised and delighted' on seeing pictures of crowns and royal emblems designed in her honour during a short visit to the town. In addition to greeting important visitors 'Sanding' still plays a part in the local traditional May Day celebrations.

The annual procession passes through the decorated streets with their sanded pavements. The queen, her maids of honours, and the ceremonial sword bearer, walk together with representations of such figures as Robin Hood and Maid Marian. Even the local highwayman Edward Higgins joins the characters assembled on Knutsford Heath. Another sinister personage is Jack-in-the-green, a man dressed in a wicker cage deco-rated with flowers and greenery, showing only his eyes and feet as he capers about with the Morris dancers. Like Jack, the Morris men are believed to be symbolic of ancient fertility rites when human blood had to be spilt to ensure the success of the crops.

A familiar sight in Victorian times, the chimney sweeps were able to enjoy a well-earned day off to join the procession. The origin of their link to May Day celebrations is unknown, but they would walk each year, carrying their shovels which they would bang for attention.

Until the various 19th century Acts had finally succeeded in outlawing the iniquitous employment of 'climbing boys', the sweeps would have been accompanied by their small apprentices. Forgetting for one day their hard and perilous existence, the urchins would cover their sooty faces with chalk, adorn their filthy rags with tinsel, and dance and sing through the streets, collecting halfpence from spectators.

In 1887 the celebrations became the 'Knutsford Royal May Day', when the then Prince and Princess of Wales attended the crowning on the Heath. History had come full circle as the future Edward VII and his wife, the Danish born Alexandra, now trod in the footsteps of her countryman Canute, observing the tradition he had bequeathed to the town.

Knutsford's May Day still proudly bears its royal title, and the sand pictures adorn the town's thoroughfares.

The Guy Fawkes
Night Tragedy

On the evening of 5th November we expect the sounds of minor explosions to disrupt the peaceful winter darkness. But in 1772 Guy Fawkes night brought tragedy, not innocent pleasure, to many Chester families.

Who would associate the knockabout comedy of Mr Punch and his long-suffering wife Judy with death and destruction? Yet that is exactly what happened when, on that fateful evening, a massive explosion devastated Eaton's Assembly Rooms during a children's puppet show.

This building, situated in an alley linking Watergate Street and Commonhall Street, was a popular venue for dancing and other pleasurable functions. Right in the heart of the city, the passageway was known as 'Puppet Show Entry' long after the events of that fateful evening, but modernisation has now eliminated all traces of the entry.

As advertised throughout Chester during the previous week the performance certainly would have sounded attractive to young Cestrians. It stated boldly:

'Mr Punch takes this method to inform Ladies and Gentlemen that he and his grand company of artificial comedies hath opened their new theatre.'

It can well be imagined that the local youngsters pleaded with their parents to be allowed to attend, and there was indeed a packed house that night.

While Punch continued his traditional ill-treatment of his

77

wife and baby and fought his battles with authority, some 800 pounds of gunpowder stored in a grocer's warehouse beneath the theatre suddenly and mysteriously ignited. Possibly it had become unstable and the reverberations from the floor above had activated it. The main force of the explosion travelled upwards, the store-room itself sustained surprisingly little damage. The remainder of the building, some 40 ft high, contained in addition to the store-room the Puppet Theatre, which was housed in a room 11 ft in height. There were two further stories each seven ft high. It was these three upper rooms that took the full force of the blast.

A nearby building was also destroyed and damage was done to property some yards away. It was reported that many city dwellers felt their homes rocked by the explosion, and tremors were experienced by those residing in the suburbs some several miles distant.

The list of casualties was extensive, among them about 40 fatalities, mainly the children who made up most of the audience. The Royal Infirmary, fortunately situated quite near the scene, admitted about 57 of the injured. There were probably others, who would either have been treated by their local practitioners, or who tended their own wounds. The sad toll of dead and injured brought tragedy to many families that night, certainly to that Chester merchant said to have gone insane after hearing that his young son and daughter had both been killed.

The horrific incident led to some heroic rescues and many acts of bravery. One local man, Thomas Townsend, regardless of his own safety rushed into the rubble of the building and dug out victims with his bare hands. Amid that awful scene of carnage Mr Townsend shouted encouragement to others to follow his example, and together they freed many of the trapped youngsters. Thomas also administered first-aid on the spot and when he could do no more, went to the hospital and gave comfort to the injured. A less admirable citizen who while viewing the dreadful sight was heard to remark: 'Is there anyone of consequence injured?'

was sent to Coventry by his fellows for some considerable time.

As the unfortunate victims were carried to hospital on the shoulders of the rescue workers one group of boys probably gave thanks for their lucky escape. These were the pupils of Mainwaring House, a nearby small private school. After tickets had been purchased for that night's performance, the master who was due to accompany them fell ill, and they were not allowed to attend unsupervised.

While the shocked citizens were still trying to come to terms with the disaster, which in fact, at that time was Britain's worst ever explosive accident, an enquiry that began on 7th November confirmed that the stored gunpowder was responsible for the dreadful accident.

Today, when places of entertainment have such stringent safety precautions it seems incredible that explosives would be kept in a public building but at that period potentially lethal storage methods were not unusual.

It was never established why the gunpowder should have ignited at that particular time, and no responsibility appears to have been attributed to any person. It was a tragic coincidence that on the night celebrating the failure of Guy Fawkes' infamous Gunpowder Plot the same substance was to be responsible for a horrific accident in the ancient city of Chester.

A Dead Man Hangs

As gruesome as it might seem to us, a public execution was once a popular and entertaining day out for the whole family. The adults would arrive early to make sure of a good spot, bringing their own food and drink, or perhaps purchasing something from the many refreshment vendors. The children would play happily while awaiting the forthcoming spectacle under the watchful gaze of their elders. Indeed it was believed that a public hanging would provide a salutary lesson to the young, demonstrating what could happen if they strayed off the straight and narrow path.

Not everyone approved of justice being seen to be done in this very barbaric way. During the late 18th and early 19th centuries a growing movement throughout the country expressed concern at the practice. Such eminent men as Sir Samuel Romilly and Robert Peel believed public hangings did nothing to deter crime, the main reason given for retaining this form of punishment.

Sentences varied greatly, and murder was by no means the only crime to carry the death penalty. In 1786, James Buckley of Chester was convicted of burglary and sentenced to hang, whereas, in 1805 John Davies received only six months and a fine of 6s 8d, with a recognizance of £100 to keep the peace, for drowning John English in the Ellesmere canal.

In Chester, the leading opponent of public execution was John Fletcher, the editor of the city's newspaper, who waged a long campaign for the removal of the town's gallows, situated at Boughton. In the early summer of 1801, Mr Fletcher and his supporters finally achieved their aim after the last public hanging had taken place on Gallows Hill.

It had been raining hard all night, but this did not deter the citizens from turning out on Saturday, 9th May, for three men were to be executed that day. Two were forgers, Samuel Thompson and John Morgan, who provoked little sympathy as they had caused ruin to a number of townsfolk. The third was different however; for John Clare was a handsome young fellow in his twenties who had been convicted of what was a relatively minor burglary. He created further interest on receiving his sentence by declaring in ringing tones that reverberated around the court room that he would never hang.

The crowds lined the route from the gaol, anticipating with undisguised excitement the appearance of the cart containing the condemned men. The road had become extremely muddy after the previous night's storm, and the vehicle made slow progress down Lower Bridge Street, Pepper Street and through the Newgate. Inside the cart stood the three men, hands tied and legs weighed down by heavy irons.

The party reached Gallows Hill, now a pleasant green area called Barrel-Well Hill. The scaffold facing them had been erected as a 'temporary' structure some ten years previously. Temporary, because the banning of public executions had been expected for some time.

These three unfortunate men were assisted from the cart by the sheriff's officers who had taken over the responsibility for the prisoners from their gaolers. The crowd pushed forward for a better view, and this gave John Clare the opportunity he had been waiting for. He pulled the ropes off his wrists and despite the restraining leg irons made a desperate bid for freedom. The crowd drew back in surprise, allowing Clare through. He fell, staggered to his feet, then fell once more. This time he rolled down the bank towards the river Dee.

The spectators chased him, greatly impeding the sheriff's men. Clare plunged into the swollen waters, and hopelessly attempted to swim to the opposite bank and safety. He managed only a few yards when, pulled down by his leg irons, the poor man drowned.

The sheriff's men now set about retrieving the body, an operation that took a full hour. Their next action horrified even the most hardened spectators who, though they had come eagerly expecting to witness death, were not totally prepared for the sight of John Clare's lifeless body being dragged to the scaffold. They watched aghast as the noose was placed around his neck, and his corpse swung from the gallows. The young man's boast that he would never hang was sadly proved untrue.

The two forgers Thompson and Morgan were forced to stand and watch these gruesome proceedings until their turn finally came. It might then have been supposed that the day's shocking occurrences were over, but this was not the case. While the bodies were being transported back to the prison for burial, the bad condition of the road and a degree of incompetence caused the driver to overturn the cart in Pepper Street, The three corpses, two of which were still warm, were flung into the road for all to see. John Clare's body was still soaking wet.

These appalling events certainly justified John Fletcher's campaign for the abolition of public executions in the city. The 'temporary' scaffold was to have been kept as a reminder to would-be criminals, but revulsion caused by the events of 9th May led to its complete removal – a fact that John Fletcher was happy to print in the *Chester Chronicle* a few days later.

Mother Redcap, the Wreckers' Friend

A s they cross the river Mersey on one of its famous ferries, visitors and commuters alike have the opportunity to gaze at the peaceful Wirral coastline. However, had they been on the river some stormy night 200 years ago, those shores would have been far from inviting.

For those were the days when wreckers plied their evil trade. Unsuspecting ships would be lured on to the treacherous rocks by men displaying lanterns which the sailors mistook for the safety of a lighthouse. Any member of the crew or passenger who survived the sinking of the vessels were likely to be cruelly dispatched by the ruthless raiders, whose one aim was to get their hands on valuable cargoes which traditionally they could not do while there was even one survivor of the wreck. Smuggling too was rife, the part-time occupation of fishermen, labourers and small farmers who landed cargoes of dutiable goods such as brandy, tobacco and tea at secluded coves along the coast.

Once having got their booty ashore smugglers and wreckers both, needed a safe haven to hide the goods. In this Mother Redcap, a Wallasey innkeeper, was of invaluable service to her neighbours. Described as a 'comely, fresh-coloured Cheshire-spoken woman' who always wore a red hood, she was the trusted confidante of the smugglers in the late 18th and early 19th centuries. Illicit goods were taken under cover of darkness to her premises and hidden from the revenue officers. She also held amounts of cash for her customers.

The inn was situated between Caithness and Lincoln Drive on the edge of Liscard Moor, just above the high water mark. Originally built as a house in the 16th century it had later been converted into a tavern, and had long been a place of intrigue. At one time it was used by Jacobite supporters to pass messages, and one such letter, concealed in a tin of tobacco, almost caused the discovery of this safe house. A customs officer on finding what he believed were illegal goods said he would keep quiet for half the contents. After the letter had been discreetly removed he was presented with the half-filled tin.

During Mother Redcap's tenancy on the pebbled foreshore in front of the inn there was a wooden bench made of old ships' timbers. At the end of this was a flagpole topped by a weather vane. This was not what it appeared however, but merely camouflage for its true purpose. The figure of a cock was firmly secured to the flagpole, which was then fitted into a wooden socket in the shingle. The pole could then be turned to give a prearranged signal; when the vane pointed to the house it meant all was clear for the smugglers to enter, but if it faced away towards the river, then the customs officers were in the area.

There was also another more lethal obstruction for the unwary revenue men. Once inside the five inch thick studded front door the unwanted visitor had an unpleasant surprise; the floor boards were constructed on a swivel principle, held in place by a locking device. If the door was forced open the bolt of the trap was automatically pulled back, plunging the unsuspecting visitor into the cellar. This secret room was also used for the storage of looted goods.

The wreckers and smugglers trusted Mother Redcap implicitly, for not only was she the guardian of their loot, she had also saved them from capture on many occasions. It was her clever ruse that helped a group of men successfully move a cargo of rum one windswept night when a lone revenue officer was patrolling outside the tavern.

This enterprising lady sent one of the smugglers down to

the shore to lie down in the water at the edge of the receding tide. Another of the gang ran to the officer and told him that a drowned man had been washed up on the shore. The man hurried to do his duty, and down at the water's edge began searching the 'body' for means of identification. Suddenly, the 'corpse' sprang into life and knocked the revenue man unconscious with a single violent blow. By the time he recovered, the rum literally had been spirited away. The 'drowned' man later excused himself to the authorities by saying that while walking along the shore he had suffered a fit. Recovering to find a stranger searching his pockets, he had believed the man was robbing him and had retaliated accordingly.

When a ship ran aground through the work of the local wreckers another of Mother Redcap's ploys to foil the law proved just as successful. The officers spotted two men running from the stricken ship, each carrying a small bale and heading in the direction of Wallasey. They chased the fugitives for some distance only to find when the men were finally caught that the packets contained only cabbage leaves. The cargo of tobacco had been moved by other members of the gang while the officers were occupied chasing the men acting as decoys.

Despite their suspicions the government men could not prove Mother Redcap's involvement. It could be that they did not try too hard, as they too were her customers, often to be seen drinking her famous strong dark home-brewed ale. And of course the close-lipped community would betray nothing that threatened their lucrative business. For smuggling and wrecking was a way of life; demonstrated by such incidents as the appearance of the majority of the neighbourhood ladies in dresses of similar fine material. This happened shortly after the loss of a vessel loaded with silk.

The inn survived long after the death of Mother Redcap, and the end of such lawless activity along the Wirral shoreline. It later became a popular café, with a sign displaying a likeness of the lady herself holding a frying-pan.

Below the picture was the following verse:

> 'All ye that are weary come in and take rest,
> Our eggs and our ham they are of the best
> Our ale and our porter are likewise the same,
> Step in if you please and give 'em a name.'

The building sadly became derelict in the 1960s, and was finally demolished some years later. Some say however that on a wild winter night shadowy figures can be seen near the shore, the shades of men returning to claim their goods, for as Mother Redcap had died suddenly she was unable to disclose the whereabouts of valuables in her safe keeping. It may be that a considerable fortune still waits to be found.

The Imperial Huntress

The green and pleasant lands of Cheshire have long echoed to the sound of the huntsman's horn. Since the time of the first Norman earl, mighty Hugh Lupus – 'Gros Veneur', or 'Great Hunter' – many notable people have followed the hounds across the fields of the county. Indeed Cheshire boasts England's oldest surviving hunt club, founded in 1762 at Tarporley.

With such a background it is not surprising that the Empress Elizabeth of Austria chose to pursue her favourite sport in this part of the country. Tiring of curious onlookers in Hungary, where she had been introduced to the sport, the wife of Franz Josef first came to England to hunt in 1876. While hunting at Althorp on the estate of Earl Spencer, Elizabeth, or 'Sisi' as she was affectionately known, first met Captain 'Bay' Middleton, a man who was to play an important role in her life. The gallant captain had the job of riding ahead of the empress, picking the safest paths to take and places to jump.

Elizabeth then enjoyed several seasons hunting in Ireland with her devoted captain but her husband fearing for her safety in that country's unstable political situation, curtailed her visits. It was then that 'Sisi's' private secretary, Herr Linger, who had previously been employed in Cheshire, suggested try this area for the season of 1881.

As Lord and Lady Combermere were planning to visit the West Indies to view property, they readily agreed to lease their home, Combermere Abbey on the Cheshire/Shropshire border, to the empress from mid February to late March. The rent was a mere £600, but the house did require some improvements to make it acceptable to its royal resident. The doors were heightened, wiring was installed to accommodate an electric bell system, and Brown's, Chester's exclusive department store, supplied furniture and carpets.

The dressing-room next to the royal bedroom was fitted up as a gymnasium, with wall bars and a trapeze. It seems the imperial lady was ahead of her time in her love of exercise and quest for physical fitness; indeed Elizabeth, now in her early forties, was still a beautiful woman who took a great pride in her appearance.

When the alterations had been completed at a cost to the emperor of £10,000, his wife arrived at Wrenbury station where a special waiting-room had been built to accommodate Elizabeth and her entourage of 80. To ensure all went smoothly for the imperial train's journey, the top-hatted station-master from Crewe had joined the party at Euston. All went well, and a large crowd turned out to greet the visitors, amongst them was Captain Middleton, who had arrived earlier to finalise arrangements for the empress's horses.

The day after her arrival Elizabeth was out hunting with a meet from Adderley Hall, but her fellow participants must have needed considerable patience. Before the empress took to the field a tailor came specially from Whitchurch to sew the skirt of her blue cloth riding habit to its tightly-fitted bodice so that there was no wrinkling around her 18 inch waist. She also underwent an elaborate skin care routine during which a lotion comprising camphor, borax and crushed wild strawberries mixed with vaseline was applied to her face. This was Elizabeth's own recipe for preserving her perfect complexion. Tanks of sea-water were also brought from the North Wales coast to provide for her bathing. As she was always conscious of her figure, diet too was important, and a bowl of broth was all the breakfast Elizabeth would take before she finally took to the field.

The first hunt proved unsuccessful as the fox escaped, having swum the lake at Combermere. Undeterred, on the following day the empress joined a hunt at Cholmondeley. On this occasion the *Chester Chronicle* described her as the 'finest horsewoman in Europe. She is tall, a brunette in complexion, with a figure that is simply divine, lithe as a willow, and her every movement as she guides her horse with consummate skill is graceful in the extreme'. It was also said by fellow hunter Sir Watkin Williams-Wyn that she 'looked like an angel and rode like the devil'.

The lovely 'Sisi' enchanted the gentlemen with both her looks and her riding skills. She also inspired the poet laureate of the Tarporley Hunt Club, Sir Rowland Egerton Warburton, to dedicate his final work to her. Now blind, Sir Rowland was famed for his *Hunting Songs*, and his last, 'A Cheshire Welcome', was penned in the empress's honour.

Despite reportedly finding the jumping in Cheshire inferior to that in Ireland, Elizabeth returned the following year. The local gentry again welcomed their noble guest, and she was once more reunited with Captain Middleton. But the ladies of Cheshire did not invite her to visit them in their homes; they were obviously somewhat put out by the fact that during the previous year only their menfolk were asked to Combermere in return for their hospitality.

During Sisi's second and final visit Lord Combermere had been resident at the smaller Bunbury House, and on her departure she presented him with a gold snuff-box set with diamonds. The empress also showed generosity to those who served her; the butler and housekeeper received a piece of jewellery each, and the Crewe station-master was given shirt-studs and cuff-links. While hunting Elizabeth had kept a number of lace handkerchiefs which she would give to people who opened gates for her.

'Sisi' never returned to hunt in England after the season of 1882. Apparently this was also the end of her friendship with 'Bay' Middleton who, like his beloved empress, was to meet a tragic end, for he was killed in a fall at a point to point meeting in 1892. Six years later, while visiting Geneva, his royal riding companion was assassinated by an anarchist.

A Cheshire 'Chief'

Situated beside the river Bollin, Macclesfield has been associated with the textile industry since Charles Roe opened the first silk mill in 1756. Such employment was not to everyone's taste however. Some of the local young men, like William Buckley for instance, craved more excitement than a career in the mills or on the land could offer.

When he was about 20, young William, an impressive figure some 6ft 6ins tall, volunteered for the British Army in his search for adventure. The army must have welcomed this fine strapping young chap, and at the beginning of the 19th century he was posted to Gibraltar. But the strict discipline and spartan conditions endured by the troops bred discontent and William allowed himself to be influenced by dissident elements in the garrison, who drew him into a dangerous plot – to break out of barracks and murder their commanding officer.

If this plan had been successful, the course of history, not only of this country, would have been changed. For the commanding officer was Edward, Duke of Kent, the fourth son of George III, later to become the father of a daughter destined to rule an empire – Victoria.

The revolt failed, and the men were captured and tried for mutiny. The ringleaders were shot, but William and others who had played a lesser part were sentenced to transportation to Australia. In 1803, on arrival at Port Phillip, which later became Melbourne, Buckley and three other convicts escaped from their guards. During the breakout one of the men was shot, but the others made off into the bush.

After a disagreement his two fellow escapees deserted

Buckley, leaving him alone in the outback with nothing more than a tin mug and a kettle. He was a resourceful man however, and after building a rough shelter he set out in search of food.

Before he had gone far William came across a grave from which protruded a metal spear. Thinking this would be useful for killing game, and was of no further use to the deceased, the fugitive took the weapon and continued his quest. Soon he met a party of aborigines, from whom he learned that the grave was that of their late chief. The tribesmen, to whom this enormous white man seemed like a god, thought their leader had been reincarnated, a belief that was reinforced when they saw he carried their chief's ceremonial spear.

The tribesmen took William Buckley back to their village where he was accepted without question as the new leader. They clothed him in the traditional kangaroo skin robe of a chief, and taught him their language and customs.

For 32 years William Buckley neither saw another white face nor had any contact with civilization until the day several of his 'subjects' returned from a hunting expedition and produced pocket handkerchiefs. Buckley questioned them as to where they had obtained these and learnt the men had come across the camp of John Batman, who had arrived from Van Dieman's Land (Tasmania) to establish what later became the city of Melbourne. The two Englishmen met, and Batman helped his fellow countryman regain his language and re-enter the society he had left so many years before. Buckley became bodyguard to Batman in his role of Founder and colonel-in-command of the new colony.

When news reached Britain of the strange existence this son of Cheshire had lived for so long and the help he had given John Batman he was granted a pardon. William must have felt truly vindicated for past misdeeds when he was also awarded a pension which allowed him to end his days in comfort. William Buckley never returned to his Macclesfield home but died at Hobart at the ripe old age of 76.

Lady Beswick's Strange Bequest

Described by the author Thomas De Quincey as the 'most eminent surgeon in the north of England', the 18th century Sale resident Dr Thomas White must indeed have been a remarkable man. As well as running his thriving medical practice this good doctor kept a most unusual collection of specimens at his home, part of which he turned into a small private museum. This exhibition was visited by numerous people, both during White's lifetime and when the exhibition passed into other hands. Visitors during the early 19th century included De Quincey, who wrote about the experience in his *Autobiographic Sketches* (1834 - 41).

The strangest exhibit he would have seen would have been undoubtedly the mummified body of Lady Beswick, a very wealthy former patient of Dr White. This lady was somewhat of an eccentric, and also a chronic hypochondriac. White had been her physician for a considerable period, during which he frequently had been forced to listen to a catalogue of her many phobias, the oddest of which was her fear of being buried prematurely. It was for this reason Lady Beswick charged her doctor with the task of making sure she was not placed below ground until 100 years after her death.

When in 1757 the elderly woman finally succumbed to an ailment that was not imaginary, Thomas White discovered he had been left £25,000 in her will. This was an extremely large sum of money for the period, and although the conditions were unusual, he happily adhered to them.

Lady Beswick was by her own request embalmed by the 'best techniques of London and Paris', then placed in a glass-fronted grandfather clock case, with a piece of white velvet as a veil to cover her face. This highly original coffin was then placed on the roof of Dr White's home at Sale.

In accordance with the terms of the will once a year the doctor and two other witnesses removed the veil and inspected the corpse, presumably to make sure she had not returned to life in the past twelve months, highly unlikely as this seems after the embalming process! On the demise of Thomas White in 1776 this duty, together with the remaining fortune passed to his former pupil and colleague, Dr Ollier.

In addition to the yearly viewings, many privileged visitors who like De Quincey had an interest in the bizarre and unusual came to see Lady Beswick and the other exhibits. Among these was a skeleton that Thomas White had procured, declaring it to be that of an 'infamous Cheshire highwayman'. De Quincey, among many others believed it to be the remains of none other than 'Gentleman Higgins', the Knutsford highwayman, house burglar and murderer, hanged in Carmarthen in 1767, whose story appears in an earlier chapter.

This could not be proved however, as another medical man, a Dr Lupton discovered when he made inquiries in 1814. At this time Dr Ollier was in charge of the exhibits, but could not confirm the skeleton was that of Higgins.

After Dr Ollier's death the collection passed into the safe keeping of the Manchester Natural History Society's own museum. They in turn presented the exhibits to the trustees of Owen's College (later Manchester University). It seems possible that the skeleton, be it Higgins or some other criminal, ended up as a visual aid for the anatomy class.

Lady Beswick was treated with more respect however. When the college took possession of her embalmed body in 1868, it was decided that at long last she should be given a Christian burial. This took place on 22nd July of that year at Harpurhey cemetery in Manchester. That determined lady's careful plans had achieved what she desired and more – for she had succeeded in remaining above ground for 111 years.

Selected Bibliography

Cheshire Curiosities Peter Bamford (Dovecote Press)

The Illustrated Portrait of Wirral Kenneth Burnley (Robert Hale)

Cheshire Village Book Cheshire Federation of Women's Institutes
   (Countryside Books)

Cheshire Fred H. Crossley (Robert Hale)

Romantic Cheshire J. Cumming Walters (Hodder & Stoughton)

Cheshire R. N. Dore (B. T. Batsford)

The Wirral Peninsular Norman Ellison (Robert Hale)

Discovering Cheshire Ron and Marlene Freethy (John Donald)

Knutsford, its History Henry Green (E. J. Morten)

The Chester Mystery Plays Maurice Hussey (Heinemann)

The Great Fire of Nantwich Jeremy Lake (Shiva)

Delamere ed. Frank A. Latham (Local History Group)

Myths and Legends of Chester A. E. Marshall MRSH MIST (Chester
   Blind Welfare Society)

Arthur Mee's Cheshire (Hodder & Stoughton)

The Treasures of Cheshire (North West Civic Trust)

Picturesque Cheshire Roger Oldham (Methuen)

Mysterious Cheshire Philip Rickman (Dalesman Books)

Shakespeare's Sonnets A. L. Rowse (Macmillan)

Cheshire Gleanings E. A. Williams (Tubb, Brook & Chrystal)

Chester B. C. A. Windle (Methuen)

Legends and Traditions of Cheshire Frederick Woods (Shiva)

Further Legends and Traditions of Cheshire Frederick Woods (Shiva)